STRATEGY

FOR

SUCCESSFUL

LIVING

A GUIDE ON HOW TO DISCOVER AND LIVE OUT YOUR LIFE PURPOSE

Solomon chikan

CONTENTS

1. WHAT THIS BOOK IS ALL ABOUT AND WHY I HAVE WRITTEN IT...........................2

2. WHAT YOUR LIFE REALLY IS.......................................10

3. WHAT A SUCCESSFUL LIFE IS.......................................22

4. HOW A SUCCESSFUL LIFE IS LIVED AND ACHIEVED........38

5. THINGS YOU MUST KNOW AND HAVE TO BE ABLE TO LIVE AND FULFILL YOUR LIFE PURPOSE IN A GOD HONORING WAY AND HAVE A SUCCESS FULL LIFE..........60

6. HOW TO LIVE AND ACQUIRE
    THE REQUIREMENTS FOR A
    SUCCESSFUL LIFE 78

7. HOW TO DISCOVER YOUR
    GOD ORDAINED LIFE
    PURPOSE OR CALLING.......98

8. WHY YOU NEED TO LIVE AND
    FULFILL YOUR LIFE
    PURPOSE..........................114

9. HOW TO ACQUIRE THE
    REQUIREMENTS THAT A
    PERSON NEEDS TO LIVE AND
    FULFILL HIS LIFE
    PURPOSE..........................120

1:00 WHAT THIS BOOK IS ALL ABOUT AND WHY I HAVE WRITTEN IT.

I am a life coach and in the course of my work, I have had to speak in many seminars and conferences and I have in these seminars and conferences been asked many questions about life, its purpose, how a person can discover his life purpose and how a person can live to fulfill it. I have also listened to many people talk and complain about issues that they are facing in life which they believe are responsible for why their lives have not turned out to be what they would have wanted them to be.

As I reflected on all these questions that I have been asked in the various seminars, workshops and conferences that I have spoken in and the things that I have listened to in my private coaching sessions, it seems clear to me that the number one issue that most people are facing in life which has made their lives not be what they would have wanted them to be is their inability to know what their God ordained life purposes or callings are and where they know them, how they are to live and fulfill them.

This discovery did not come to me as a surprise as, books that have been written about life, its purpose and what a purposeful life is, have sold millions of copies. One of such books is **The purpose driven life** by Rick Warren which I learnt has sold more than fifteen million copies and is still selling. Rick Warren in the opening pages of the book gave the reason for his writing the book as wanting to help people answer life's most important question, which is, **"what on earth am I here for?"** I agree with him that this is life's most important question and people should be helped to answer the question and answer it correctly, but I think just helping people to know why they are here in the World is not enough. I believe that, after they have been helped to

discover why they are here in
the world there is also the need
for them to be helped to know
how they are to live and fulfill it.

This book titled **STRATEGY
FOR SUCCESSFUL LIVING**
has been written to serve as a
guide for people on how they
can discover and live out their
God ordained life purposes in a
God honoring way. The book
explains in very simple
language what a persons God
ordained life purpose is, how a
person can discover it and how
he is to live and fulfill it. The
book also explains how a
person can find and create what
to do to be able to live out his
life purpose. As I said earlier
most of the books that have
been written on the subject of

life and its purpose only tell people that life has a purpose and what the purpose is in general terms but few go further to tell them how they can discover and live out their own God ordained individual purposes. How a person can discover his personal life purpose, how to live and fulfill it and why he should and must live to fulfill it are not usually focused at and explained hence they are not known by most people. The knowledge of how a person can discover his life's God ordained purpose and how to live and fulfill it has been a missing link in most people's effort to live life successfully. This book has therefore been written to provide this missing link, it explains how a person can discover his individual God ordained life purpose, how such a person can find, create and do what can enable him live and fulfill it and why he should and must seek to live and fulfill it.

If you have been searching for how to discover your life purpose and how to live and fulfill it, then search no further as this book will enable you to do that. It will also help you to know how to find what to do to fulfill it and why you must and should seek to be able to live and fulfill your life purpose.

The book has been written for the sole purpose of providing the many people like you who have been searching for how to live life successfully and have been asking questions about how they can do it with the answers to the following questions which they have been asking ;

(i) What is my life purpose or calling ?

(ii) How do I discover it ?

(iii) How do I live to fulfill it ?

(iv) What do I do to fulfill it ?

(v) How do I find what to do to fulfill it?

(vi) Why should I live to fulfill my life purpose or calling and in a God honoring way?

2:00 WHAT YOUR LIFE REALLY IS

For us to be able to know how a person can discover his God ordained life purpose and what the strategy for living and fulfilling it to have a successful life should be and what life should be about for an individual, we will need to know what life really is. It is only when we know what life really is can we arrive at how to live it correctly. I will therefore want us to start our journey to how you can discover and live out your life purpose with the question;

what really is your life?

Going by what we read in the
Bible, we can say that every life
is,

(a) a trust,

This means your life is not yours
and as such it is not to be used
anyhow by you as a trust is
given for a purpose and will
have to be accounted for. Your
life is therefore on loan to you
and you are only a manager or
a steward of it . Given these
facts about life, it means life
must and should be cared for,
preserved and used only for its
purpose by a possessor of life.
Life must and it should be cared
for and stewarded faithfully
because a day is coming when
it will have to be accounted for

by its possessors to the owner and giver. This is why it is said that a steward is expected to be faithful and should be faithful. Every person who is a steward must heed this advice because studies have revealed that there are bad consequences that follow poor or unfaithful stewardship even before the day of accountability. **Luke 16:1-2,10-12** which I quote below brings out very clearly these bad consequences of unfaithfulness in stewardship.

" Jesus told his disciples: "There was a rich man whose manager was accused of wasting his possessions. So he called him in and asked him, 'What is this I hear about you? Give an account of your management, because

*you cannot be manager any
longer.' ....*

*"Whoever can be trusted with
very little can also be trusted
with much, and whoever is
dishonest with very little will also
be dishonest with much. So if
you have not been trustworthy in
handling worldly wealth, who
will trust you with true riches?
And if you have not been
trustworthy with someone else's
property, who will give you
property of your own?"*

(b) a promise

Every human being comes to
the world as God's answer to a
human cry for the solution to an
existing human problem or as
a solution to a human problem

that is yet to manifest. This makes every life including yours a prophecy and a gift. These truths confirm the fact that every human being is a gift from God to His children in the world as a means for the fulfillment of His promise and responsibility as a father to meet all the needs of His children. This means, when a person is not able to live and solve the human problem he came into the world for, he becomes an un fulfilled promise, a bad gift and this makes God to be seen as a liar, a father who is un able to meet the needs of his children and as such a father who does not care about his children.

When a person is able to live and fulfill his God ordained life purpose he makes the world a better place and makes people to honor and thank God always. Satan does not want this to happen hence he is working hard daily to make sure that every person born in the world does not get to live out his life purpose. He is doing this through, keeping people in ignorance, distractions which come to people through being busy in things that are not their lives purposes.

(c)   An opportunity ,

(i) For training and testing to be made worthy of heaven.

(ii)To partner with God to maintain the earth(work it and keep it).

(iii)To partner with God to reclaim the lost.

(iv) For fulfilling the promise that the life is.

The fact that life is an opportunity means that life has a duration, it does not last forever. Every human being has been given a period of time to live on earth and during this period he is expected to fulfill the promise that he is. For man to be continuously reminded of this fact that his life has a duration and every passing day and moment brings him closer to the end of his life just like a burning candle which becomes shorter and shorter as it burns, man has been created in a way that he deteriorates physically and he becomes weaker as he gets older(spends more time on the earth).If a person can from time to time withdraw from the busyness of life and take time to reflect about his life and take a good look at himself he will be able to see that his life and indeed his time on earth is coming to the end with each passing day as he can see how his physical make up is changing and deteriorating and he is becoming weaker and weaker. This will enable him to know that every passing day and moment is a counting down in his life .

King David in the Bible knew this truth that life has hence the advice he has given in Psalms 90:10,12 which says,

"The days of our lives are seventy; and if by reason of strength they are eighty years, yet their boast is only labor and sorrow for it is soon cut off and we fly away........,so teach us to number our days that we may gain a heart of wisdom"

These things that I have listed and explained above bring out very clearly the fact that life like all other things that God makes available to people does not belong to the possessor, it is a trust and He will expect every possessor of life as all other things that He makes available, to steward it faithfully and give account of it at its end. Every possessor of anything that comes from God should see himself therefore as a steward and live as such.

Matthew 25:14-19, which I have quoted below further confirms and brings out this truth that God does not give things but He entrusts and He expects those He entrusts things to, to give account of how they have used them when He returns.

"Again, it will be like a man going on a journey, who called his servants and entrusted his property to them. To one he gave five talents of money, to another two talents, and to

another one talent, each according to his ability. Then he went on his journey. The man who had received the five talents went at once and put his money to work and gained five more. So also, the one with the two talents gained two more. But the man who had received the one talent went off, dug a hole in the ground and hid his master's money.

After a long time the master of those servants returned and settled accounts with them. "

3:00 WHAT IS A SUCCESSFUL LIFE ?

Permit me to continue our discussion of how a person can discover his God ordained life purpose, how to live and fulfill it and why each of us should seek to know his individual life purpose and live to fulfill it by asking the following two questions,

what is success and what is a successful life?

Did I hear you ask what has knowing the answers to these questions got to do with our subject? Studies have revealed that answering these questions will enable us to know why every person needs to discover his live purpose and must seek to live and fulfill it and how knowing and being able to do these will result in a person having a successful life.

Success is said to have been achieved or is being achieved when an activity planned and embarked upon is carried out and the purpose or reason for which the activity was planned is achieved or is being achieved. In the case of a product, success is said to have been achieved when the product is able to serve the purpose for which it has been made.

Studies revealed that when purpose is not known, be it for an activity or a product abuse is eminent and success will not be achieved in the activity or in the use of the product. It is because of this that, the first requirement for achieving success especially for any activity a person wants to embark upon is that, the person that is the doer of the activity must know what the activity really is and why the activity is being done or what the activity is all about before even trying to know how it should be done.

 From our definitions and explanations of what success and life really are, it can be said that, **a successful life can simply be defined as a life whose God ordained purpose or calling is known and it is being lived out in a God honoring way.** Success for a

life is therefore possible only
when such a life is being lived
in such a way that it is being
used for doing what enables
the purpose of the life to be
achieved in a God honoring
way. This means that, it is
possible for a person to live and
have a successful life only when
the person knows his God
ordained life purpose,
develops himself and acquires
the knowledge, personal
qualities and competencies that
enables him to live and do in a
God honoring way what
produces the value that enables
him fulfill his God ordained life
purpose. This is because,
studies revealed that all lives
purposes lived out or fulfilled

results in the creation of value for people.

With what I have said above about what a successful life is and how it is achieved, I believe you now know why even though this book is about how a person can discover and live out his life purpose it has been titled, **Strategy for successful living.** A successful life is the result of being able to discover and live out life purpose as ordained by God in a God honoring way.

To live life in a God honoring way is to live life at Gods terms and be doing what the life has been created by God for in a way that pleases and honors God. Studies revealed that life can be lived God's way only if it is being lived in partnership with God the creator of life for the fulfillment of its God ordained purpose. It is only when this is being done by a person that he can experience a truly successful life which is usually marked by satisfaction, meaning, genuine and true fulfillment. A life lived this way experiences success in life and living and it is marked by satisfaction, meaning, genuine and true fulfillment because the two vacuums that exist in a man's life which makes or leaves a person unfulfilled in life and searching unless they are filled correctly as he lives get filled when a person lives this way. The two vacuums are,

the God vacuum which is filled only by God and **the purpose vacuum** which gets filled only when a person lives and does what he has been created to do in a God honoring way. It may interest you to know that success in life and success in living are two different things but a person can live and have a successful life only when he is successful in life and living.

Success in life is generally judged in terms of the possession of material things like money or position or reputation or eminence in some particular branch of business or profession, while success in living is a very different matter. Success in living is not about the accumulation of material things or the satisfaction of appetites or ambitions, its achievement by a person can be measured only by the persons interior satisfactions which are a product of a peaceful soul. A peaceful soul results from being healthy mentally and emotionally. Studies have revealed that when a person is able to live and have his God and purpose vacuums filled correctly, he will be able to live and have success in life and living resulting in him having a successful life.

You will observe that in the above definition of what a successful life is and how it is achieved that, there is no word, phrase or activity which makes a successful life which is a product of, success in life and living and how they are achieved a competition as most people today see and live life. This brings out and confirms the fact that life is not a competition and as such having a successful life is not about winning and losing. Life is rather a race that every one involve in it can win or can succeed. Whether a person will succeed or loose in the race of life is not dependent on whether others involved in the race have won or lost; it is dependent only on the person understanding the race, which is life , its purpose, how it should be run(lived) and he develops himself and acquire the personal qualities and competencies he needs to manage and order himself to run it correctly. This is the only thing that can enable a person to run the race of life correctly and when the race comes to the end he will be declared a winner along with all others that have run the race correctly.

There is a story I was told by a friend, I don't know the source or truth of the story but it brings out very clearly these truths which I have tried to explain above about what the race of life is all about and how it should be run by a person to win or be a success.

The story has it that a man found three young boys playing in an open field. He said, "boys do you want to play a game? Each of you stand to win a prize if you win." The boys on hearing this said, " yes we will ,what's the game?" He said, "I will go and stand at the other end of the field and who ever gets to me in the most straight line wins a prize."He went and stood on the other end of the field and at his command he told the boys to start coming to him. The boys started walking and running towards him ,but it was discovered that how each walked or ran towards him varied. Each walked or ran towards him in his own way depending on how he saw and understood the race to be! The first boy saw and understood the race as a competition and as such he thinks he will get a prize only if he gets to the man before the other two boys. He was therefore focused only at getting to the man before the other two boys, he did not remember and take into consideration the instruction of the man that he will give a prize to the one that reaches him in the most straight line. He reached the man first but in a zigzag way, his path was not straight and this made him to be told by the man you have not won, you do not qualify for a prize. You get a prize only if you got to me in a straight line the man told the boy. The second boy on his part understood that the race was not a competition but he felt for him to be able to run the race and win he will have to be perfect and so as he walked towards the man he tried to get his legs as straight as possible, he believes it is only when his legs are straight that he can walk in a straight line. Unfortunately for him he had k-legs and as he constantly looked down to make sure his legs were straight as he walked and ran towards the man he could not maintain a straight line and as such could not reach the man in a straight line, he also was told by the man you failed, so there is no prize for you .To win and get a prize you must get to me in a straight line and you have not. The third boy however understood the race, he knew it was not about him getting to the man first, neither was it about his weaknesses, it was about getting to the man in a straight line. So as he started the race he kept his attention focused on the man; he was not bothered about getting to the man before the other boys or his weaknesses and this enable him to be focused and he got to him in the most straight path and he got a prize.

This story brings out the fact that life is a race but it is not a competition to seek to beat others to win. Success in the race of life is neither determined by the lack of weaknesses either. It is a race which is to be run by each of us by focusing on our individual God ordained purpose in partnership with God. With the correct knowledge of life and being in partnership with God you can win the race despite your weaknesses; God knows why He created you with them. With His help you can overcome them and win in life if you know what your life is all about, what to do to become a person who can live and fulfill it and how to live and do it successfully and you live and do them.

From the above explanations I am sure it is clear to you that life can be lived successfully by any person but it is dependent on the person knowing what life really is, knowing his particular calling, acquiring the personal qualities and competencies that gives him capacity and ability to be able to live, discipline and manage himself and do what enables him to fulfill his God ordained life purpose in a God honoring way. When a person has the capacity and ability to discipline, manage and order himself to live correctly and do what he has been created for he will succeed in life and living thereby have a successful life.

4:00 How a Successful Life is Lived and Achieved.

Given what I have discussed and explained above as what makes for a successful life, what do you think a person's life should be about? What should a person's life and indeed yours be used for ?What are you supposed to be doing with your life as you live for it to be a success?

Based on what life really is and what we have discussed in the last chapter about what a successful life is we can say that,

   (a)Life is not and should not be about things. Life and living should therefore not be about the accumulation of

things. What we read in **Luke 12:15** which says, " *Then he said to them, "Watch out! Be on your guard against all kinds of greed; a man's life does not consist in the abundance of his possessions."*

 confirms this truth that life is not about things. When life is seen and lived only for the accumulation of things, then it ends up becoming a pursuit and an appetite that can never be achieved or satisfied especially by a fallen man who is controlled by greed. Another problem that faces a person who does not know that life is not about things is that, he sees life as a competition. A competition is an activity which must produce winners and losers, therefore when life is seen and lived this way by a person, it usually ends up being full of frustrations. This is because any life that is lived this way leaves the person striving to accumulate more things than all others and this is not possible as there is always someone having more of whatever you are looking for. Life is not about being better than others or having more things than them. It is neither a competition which ends up as an effort to beat others to be a winner and not a loser.

(b)Life is not about survival (preserve it and stay alive) and as such it should not be seen and lived as a struggle for survival. When life is seen and lived as a struggle for survival it becomes very "hard." This is because it is difficult to live life and enjoy it when the focus is on survival. What was told the one talent man who did not trade with his talent but hid it (preserved it) and returned it as he was given to his master in the parable of the talents confirms this truth that life is not and should not be about survival.

The parable as found in **Matthew 25:14-30** is as follows,

"Again, it will be like a man going on a journey, who called his servants and entrusted his property to them. To one he gave five talents of money, to another two talents, and to

another one talent, each according to his ability. Then he went on his journey. The man who had received the five talents went at once and put his money to work and gained five more. So also, the one with the two talents gained two more. But the man who had received the one talent went off, dug a hole in the ground and hid his master's money.

After a long time the master of those servants returned and settled accounts with them. The man who had received the five talents brought the other five. 'Master,' he said, 'you entrusted me with five talents. See, I have gained five more.'

His master replied, 'Well done, good and faithful servant! You have been faithful with a few things; I will put you in charge of many things. Come and share your master's happiness!'

"The man with the two talents also came. 'Master,' he said, 'you entrusted me with two talents; see, I have gained two more.'

"His master replied, 'Well done, good and faithful servant! You have been faithful with a few things; I will put you in charge of many things. Come and share your master's happiness!'

"Then the man who had received the one talent came. 'Master,' he said, 'I knew that you are a hard man, harvesting where you have not sown and *gathering where you have not scattered seed. So I was afraid and went out and hid your talent in the ground. See, here is what belongs to you.'*

His master replied, 'You wicked, lazy servant! So you knew that I harvest where I have not sown and gather where I have not scattered seed? Well then, you should have put my money on deposit with the bankers, so that when I returned I would have received it back with interest.

Take the talent from him and give it to the one who has the ten talents. For everyone who has will be given more, and he will have an abundance. Whoever does not have, even what he has will be taken from him. And throw that worthless servant outside, into the darkness, where there will be weeping and gnashing of teeth."

This parable brings out very clearly what life should be about for it to be a success. The parable has clearly brought out the fact that life should be about the creation and profitable trading of value. Studies have however revealed that, for a person to be able to live, create and trade value profitably the person will have to **become** a person who can. Becoming a person who can create and trade value profitably is all about the person developing himself and acquiring the requirements that a person needs to be able to live ,create and trade value profitably. These requirements are the personal qualities and competencies(capacity and ability) that can enable him to be able to live, create and trade value profitably. For such a person to be able to live and continue to do this throughout the duration of his life, he will have to be continuously engaged in learning and growing through training in self development to remain competent and able to manage and order himself to live, create and trade value profitably. Training and development are necessary because all humans are born equipped with what they need to be able to live and create the value that they are

created for but not qualified.
Training develops them and
makes them qualified to create
and trade profitably the value
that they have been created for.

It is clear from what I have
explained above about life and
indeed living that a successful
life is that which is being used
for the fulfillment of its God
ordained purpose in a God
honoring way and as such we
can say that life and living for a
person should be about finding
and doing what can enable him
acquire the personal qualities
and competencies(abilities)
that make up the requirements
that can enable him have the
capacity and skills that he
needs to discipline and manage
himself to be able to live and do

what can enable him fulfill his God ordained life purpose in a God honoring way. However, since humans are not born with these personal qualities and competencies but only the potential, a person will need to be developed to be able to acquire these personal qualities and competencies he needs to discipline, manage and order himself to be able to live and do what he needs to do to fulfill his God ordained life purpose in a God honoring way and have a successful life.

Given what we have seen as life and what we know as God's purpose for creating man as revealed in **Genesis 1:26** which says "*Then God said, "Let us make man in our image, in our* *likeness, and let them rule over the fish of the sea and the birds of the air, over the livestock, over all the earth, and over all the creatures that move along the ground."*

and what the Bible reveals to us as what God is doing with all His children as stated in **Romans 8:28-29** which says, *"And we know that in all things God works for the good of those who love him, who have been called according to his purpose. For those God foreknew he also predestined to be conformed to the likeness of his Son, that he might be the firstborn among many brothers."*

We can conclude that life and indeed living for all people should be about them,

(i)discovering and knowing their God ordained lives purposes

(ii)finding and doing things that can enable them become people that can discipline and manage themselves to live and do the things that can enable them fulfill their God ordained purposes in life in a God honoring way.

(iii)finding and doing things that will enable them create and sustain in a healthy condition the relationships that man exist in which he needs to be able to live and be who he has been

created to be and do what he
has been created to do.

(iv) knowing and doing things
that will enable them to be fit
and remain fit for living life
successfully. A person is said to
be fit for successful living if he
is physically, mentally,
emotionally and spiritually
healthy. Being in this state of
health enables a person to have
the energy and power to live
life successfully.

(v)finding, creating and doing
in a God honoring way
activities that can enable them
create the value that can enable
them fulfill their God ordained
life purposes which goes to
contribute to the fulfillment of

God's ordained purpose for all mankind.

God has ordained a purpose for all of mankind and each individual person. These truths are clearly brought out by the following verses which I have quoted below.

God's ordained purpose for mankind is stated very clearly in **Genesis 1:26** which says,

"*Then God said, "Let us make man in our image, in our likeness, and let them rule over the fish of the sea and the birds of the air, over the livestock, over all the earth, and over all the creatures that move along the ground.*"

And the fact that God has an ordained purpose for each individual person is confirmed in **Jeremiah 1:5** which says,

"Before I formed you in the womb I knew you,

before you were born I set you apart;

I appointed you as a prophet to the nations .

Studies revealed to us that Jesus Christ was able to live, become who He was created to **be** and did fully what he came into the world for, hence He is today our model of a successful person and His life a model of a successful life. It is because of this that becoming a person who can live and have a successful life is all about becoming like Jesus Christ.

From the above explanations, I am sure what you are supposed to use your life for is now very clear to you. It is clear from what I have discussed above that life and living for a person, especially the one that wants to have a successful life, should be about, " **continuous growth or self development for becoming more and more like Jesus Christ**" and **"doing" what can enable such a person to fulfill his God ordained life purpose in a God honoring way."**

This means that, for a person to be able to live and have a successful life, his life should be about him living to become a person who can do what he needs to do to fulfill his God ordained life purpose in a God honoring way and doing it since life unlike a cassette which has sides "A" and "B" and each side can be played after the other life is lived only once!

Studies however revealed that for him to be able to do this, he will have to,

(a) discover and know his God ordained life purpose.

(b) develop himself to become a person who can live a successful life. This is a person who has the personal qualities and competencies that makes a person a success prone person. Becoming a success prone person is all about becoming a person who can be successful in whatever he does. Such a person succeeds in everything he does and hence can live life successfully.

The Bible (NKJV) in **Genesis 39:1-6** which says,

" *Now Joseph had been taken down to Egypt. And Potiphar, an officer of Pharaoh, captain of the guard, an Egyptian, bought him from the Ishmaelite who had taken him down there. The Lord was with Joseph, and he was a successful man; and he was in the house of his master the Egyptian. And his master saw that the Lord was with him and that the Lord made all he did to prosper in his hand. So*

Joseph found favor in his sight, and served him. Then he made him overseer of his house, and all that he had he put under his authority. So it was, from the time that he had made him overseer of his house and all that he had, that the Lord blessed the Egyptian's house for Joseph's sake; and the blessing of the Lord was on all that he had in the house and in the field. Thus he left all that he had in Joseph's hand, and he did not know what he had except for the bread which he ate."

reveals to us who a success prone person is and what it takes for a person to be a success prone person. It is clear from what these verses are saying that a person can become success prone if God is with him. Joseph was a success prone man and could live and be successful in all he did and indeed his life because God was with him.

(c) be able to create and sustain in a healthy condition all the relationships that man exist in. This is necessary because life is lived in relationships and as such if a person cannot create and sustain in a healthy condition relationships he will not be able to live life successfully.

(d) find, select and do or create and do an activity that can enable him to live and create value that enables him to fulfill

his God ordained life purpose.
This activity can either be a job,
a business or an invention.

(e) live and carry out this
activity to create and trade
value that benefits his fellow
man profitably in a way that
honors God.

5:00 THINGS YOU MUST KNOW AND HAVE TO BE ABLE TO LIVE AND FULFILL YOUR LIFE PURPOSE IN A GOD HONORING WAY AND HAVE A SUCCESS FULL LIFE

From our discussions so far, it is clear that living to have a successful life is like building a house. The person who wants to build a successful life like building a good house will need to know certain things, be able to follow some steps and he must have in place some things which make up the requirements for building a good house. To build a house you will have to start with the foundation then the superstructure. You will need a strategy and tactics to build.

For building a successful life, a life that is successful in life and living you will need to acquire some requirements. The study of the lives of people who are known to have lived successful lives revealed that, the requirements are twofold. There are requirements for success in life and requirements for success in living.

The study reveals the requirements that a person must have for him to be able to live, fulfill his life calling and have true success in life are the following,

He must have,

(i) the knowledge of God and he must have a personal

relationship with Him through becoming and living as a member of His family. This can enable the Holy spirit to have a total control of his life and be his guide in life. He must also have in his life developed and fully manifested the fruit of the Holy spirit. A person needs to have this knowledge and relationship because no product can live and fulfill its purpose independent of its creator.

(ii)the knowledge of his God ordained life purpose (calling).

(ii) the personal qualities and competencies that enables a person to be able to live a Godly lifestyle. The possession of these enables a person to be able to manage and order himself to do what enables him to create and trade profitably value that enables him to fulfill his God ordained life purpose in a God honoring way. Being able to live a Godly life and doing what enables the person to fulfill his God ordained life purpose in a God honoring way will enable the person to also acquire the resources that he needs to meet all his basic human needs ,which a person must meet adequately to be fit and free to be able to live and do successfully what he needs to do to fulfill his God ordained life purpose in a God honoring way. Mans basic needs are his needs at the three levels that he exist. Man exist and have needs at the spiritual, soul and physical levels.

The same study revealed that the requirements for success in living which a person must have to be able to live and succeed in living are the following three things,

(i)The first of these three things is the existence or possession of **a purpose which must be the life's God ordained purpose.** It can harness in its service all of a person's powers and capacities and it should be the coordinator of all his activities. This purpose should be the center, focus and the reason behind all the things done, can be done or not done by the person. This element of a successful life is vital for success in living and indeed the success of life as a whole because if there are capacities in a person which are not being used, power is not only wasted but there is a consequent sense of frustration and unhappiness. If a person does not have a coordinating purpose which can take into its sweep all the various activities of life in his life, then his life may be full, but it will lack both direction and unity. It is the ignorance of the need for purpose and the lack of having it in life that makes many people to drift through life without much impact, results and influence and they are only content enough if life brings them a fair amount of happiness or satisfaction, and exempts them from most of its major ills. They easily slip into grooves of routine which make thought unnecessary, and they protect themselves as best as they can by some mechanism of escape, from the shock of disturbing or challenging events. Frustrations and futility have been found to beset the minds of many people and their days full of struggles for little aims and small satisfactions because of the effect of the lack of an all encompassing purpose for life. The lack of an all encompassing purpose in life by a person can make living for such a person to be likened to trying to climb a moving staircase in the wrong direction. There is plenty of effort, but in the end the person gets nowhere. The lives of most people because of the lack of an all encompassing purpose is like this and is full of strain and restlessness .

(ii) The second of these three things is **the measure to which a person's interest ceases to be self centered and is focused at the lives and service of others**. It is what the Bible calls a life of love. How much you can love others determines how successful in living you can be.

(iii) The third of these three things is **the power to handle the various experiences of life**

positively. Life is colored by what happens to us, but the success of life does depend on how we respond to these experiences and what in the long run we do with them. The things that happen to us all have the power to do something for us or within us, they can either degrade , embitter or in some way defeat the spirit. On the other hand they can enrich, discipline, deepen, and refine it. If the captain of a sailing ship has skill, there is no wind, however it may blow, that cannot be used to send the ship on its way, but on the other hand, if there is not the skill to use it, there is no wind, however favorable, that may not drive the ship on the rocks.

In the same way, power to use the varied weather of circumstances is essential in successful living. It springs from the faith that everything that happens to us can do something for us. It can in some way develop or discipline our personality.

Jesus Christ is our perfect and best example of a person who has ever lived in this World and lived a truly successful life. He is today our expert in living and a model of a truly successful person who we can refer to and learn from how to live life successfully. He succeeded in life and living.

He never had a need in His life which He could not meet for

lack of resources. He was able to meet all His basic needs adequately.

He was also successful in living. The three elements that a person must have in his life to succeed in living discussed above existed in His life. He had a purpose which possessed His whole nature and in which every power He had was awakened and used. "My meat" He said, "is to do the will of Him that sent me, and to accomplish His work."The purpose of God met Him at every point and took His life up into its movement. All He did was related to it and inspired by it, He did not evade anything that will enable Him fulfill it. Through it His whole nature was unified. In Him there

was no unresolved   conflicts or
hidden fears. There was no
sense of frustration, though His
life was cut short by His
enemies at only thirty three.
Nothing disturbed the balance
of His mind or hindered His
freedom to be Himself.

It seems almost a waste of
words to say that the life of
Jesus was the most complete
example we have of a person
who loved others and identified
with them. He was literally one
with the sick. Sympathy is a
word that has lost some of its
vital meaning in our time but
Jesus lived out every aspect of
it. When anyone was in need He
entered fully into the situation.
His whole heart and mind were
focused upon the man's trouble,

because it became immediately His own. We do not find in Him the slightest trace of self- pity or even self-concern. When He hung on the cross and the most piercing agony and pain were racking His body, His mind was not occupied with His own feelings, He actually stood in the position of those who were crucifying Him, pleading for them with God because they were blind. It was not His own pain but their sin that broke His heart as He hung there.

His power to meet all circumstances that come His way and life experiences as a whole in the way that make them work for good was also very clear in His life. He was the master of all circumstances. He knew the way to tackle all the things that happened to Him so that nothing He enjoyed or suffered ever defeated His spirit, or made Him fail in love. But more than that there was nothing that He did not turn to good, even the cross He went to turned out to be for good.

A person can live to have a successful life only if he is able to acquire and use these requirements listed above.

The question is, why is the person who is able to have these requirements able to live a successful life?

Studies revealed that people who possess these requirements are able to live successful lives because the possession of these requirements makes it possible for them to have   qualities which enables a person to have self discipline, motivation and ability, the qualities which enables a person to do what he should do when he should do it in the way that he should do it whether he feels like doing it or not. The qualities and what they enable a person to have and do, which enable such a person to be able to live a successful life are as follows ,

(i)   commitment-
This enables a person to be committed to whatever it is that he embarks upon to do. This quality is very necessary for a successful life because without it a person cannot be focused

on what he does and be able to do it successfully.

(ii) Character

The possession of an authentic character enables a person to withstand pressures that comes on a person when engaged in the race of life. The possession of an authentic character gives a person the capacity to live life successfully.

(iii) Competence

The possession of competence enables a person to have the ability to manage and order himself   and all the relationships that man exist in rightly and also be able to do what he needs to do to obtain the result needed.

The possession of these three qualities does not only enable a person to have in place the correct foundation for building a successful life but they will also enable him to be able to operate by the right strategy and tactics to build his life through carrying out his life endeavor successfully. Having these requirements will also enable a person to be able to live life in a way that he becomes fit and remains fit for the race of life. A person is said to be fit for the race of life if such a person has access to the power a person needs to live life successfully and is in a state of good health physically, mentally, emotionally, socially and spiritually. He also needs to

be financially free and
independent.

6:00 HOW TO LIVE AND ACQUIRE THE REQUIREMENTS FOR A SUCCESSFUL LIFE

It is clear from what I have discussed so far that for a person to know his God ordained life purpose, be able to live and acquire the requirements that a person needs for the faithful stewardship of his life to have a successful life, he will need to be a person who,

(i)   knows God the creator of life who has created him and ordained his life's purpose.
(ii) has accepted Jesus Christ as his Lord and savior
(iii) lives and walk in total obedience to God, His will and

in the power of the Holy Spirit;
and has developed in his life
the fruit of the Holy Spirit.
(iv) has a life plan which
enables him to live a planned
and balanced life. These will
enable him to be able to
schedule his time and practice
the spiritual and physical
disciplines that position him to
be reached by Gods grace to
be made the person who he
needs to become to be able to
do what he has been created to
do in a God honoring way.
(v) lives by the blueprint for
living in God's kingdom.

Did I hear you ask why must a
person become this person
before he can live and have the

requirements that a person needs to live a successful life?

Studies revealed that a person will have to become this person before he can live and steward his life faithfully and be able to live and have a successful life because it is only by becoming this person that he is able to possess the requirements for a successful life.

Jesus Christ was able to live His life successfully because He had all the requirements which a person needs to be able to live a successful life. Studies revealed that Jesus Christ was able to have all these requirements for a successful life and was able to live a successful life because He had

a very perfect and healthy
relationship with God His
father. He had the full measure
of the Holy spirit and He had
manifested in his life all the
attributes that the Holy Spirit
imparts to a person when He
comes into a person's life and is
able to operate fully in the
person's life without being
hindered. These personal
qualities that the Holy spirit
imparts to a person and are
able to make him a success
prone person, a person who
can live a successful life is the
fruit of the Holy Spirit.

The question is how does a
person get the Holy spirit to
come and live in his life and
have Him able to operate fully
in his life and also have His fruit

fully developed and imparted in his life?

It is in knowing this and being able to do it that a person acquires the requirements for a successful life.

For a person to have the Holy Spirit come and live in his life and be filled and controlled fully by Him, there are things he will have to do and there is a person he must become.

The first requirement is for the person to be born again. A person gets born again by accepting Jesus Christ to be his Lord and savior. Doing this will enable him to become a citizen of God's kingdom and he will have the Holy Spirit come to live in him. For such a person to be filled by the Holy Spirit and have the Holy Spirit fully operational in his life and the fruit of the Holy spirit fully developed in his life, he will have to live, walk in the spirit and not grieve and quench the Holy Spirit in his life. A person grieves the Holy spirit when he says yes to Satan when he lures him into sin and he quenches the spirit, that is prevents Him from operating in his life, developing the fruit of the spirit and manifesting God's power in his life, when he says no to God when He woos him into sanctification and service.

 Studies have revealed that there are things such a person will need to do to be able to achieve this in his life.

Prominent amongst the things that he will have to do after being born again to be able to live, walk in the spirit, not grieve or quench Him, develop in his life the fruit of the spirit and manifest Gods power are the following,

(a)For him to not grieve the spirit he must,

(i) keep away from his life anything false, deceitful or hypocritical as the Holy Spirit is a spirit of truth.

(ii) keep away from his life doubt, unbelief, distrust, worry, anxiety as the Holy Spirit is a spirit of faith.

(iii) put out of his life that which is hard, bitter, ungracious, unthankful, malicious, unforgiving or unloving as the Holy Spirit is a spirit of grace.

(iv) put out of his life anything unclean, defiling or degrading as the Holy Spirit is a spirit of holiness.

(v) not be ignorant, conceit, arrogant and foolish as the Holy Spirit is a spirit of wisdom and revelation.

(vi) put out of his life anything that is barren, fruitless, disorderly, confused and uncontrolled as the Holy Spirit is a spirit of power, love and discipline.

(vii) put out of his life anything that is indifferent, lukewarm, spiritually dull and dead as the Holy spirit is a spirit of life.

(viii) not adapt anything worldly, earthly or fleshly as the Holy Spirit is a spirit of glory.

(b)For a person to not quench the Holy Spirit it will require that he is totally yielded to the will of God in his life and to have the Holy spirit fully functional in such a person's life with the fruit of the Holy spirit fully developed and manifested in such a life. A person who is born again can live and achieve this if he can live and walk in the spirit. He will be able to do this if he determines and deliberately decides to choose to do God's will in all things and at all times, at all costs and he does it . Living this way will enable a person to be able to develop the fruit of the Holy spirit, have God's power flow through him and be able to use it. This process of developing the fruit of the spirit cannot be achieved by a person by sheer human will power. It can be achieved only with the help of what I will want to call **"spiritual will power."** Spiritual will power involves a person's will and God's power. It is the perfect mix for producing spiritual fruit. One passage in the Bible which illustrates this process is **Philippians 2:12-13** which says,

Therefore, my dear friends, as you have always obeyed — not only in my presence, but now much more in my absence — continue to work out your salvation with fear and trembling, for it is God who works in you to will and to act according to his good purpose.

Here Paul instructs the believers in Philippi to "work out your(their) salvation with fear and trembling, for it is God who works in you to will and to act according to his good purpose." This text shows us the balance of God's part and our part in the process of living and walking in the spirit. God is at work in us so that we can work it out. The Holy spirit is present in our inner lives once we become born again. He is enabling us to produce the nine characteristics of the fruit of the spirit. In a sense, He is the nine characteristics. His presence in us makes us capable of expressing these qualities. We also have a part to play. Our job is to, **" work out"** that which God is working within. This is where the tricky balance of dependence and obedience becomes critical. For example I can't love with agape love apart from Christ in me, enabling me to love that way. But the reality of love will not be expressed until, in obedience, I choose to express it in tangible ways. John in **1John3:18** which says,

" Dear children, let us not love with words or tongue but with actions and in truth."

Clearly tells us not to love in words only, but in deed and in truth. This means there is something we must do to be able to love, there is a part for us to play. You may have noticed that nearly every dimension of the fruit of the spirit is a quality about which some other part of the New Testament instructs or commands us to take action.

e.g. Jesus in **John 13:35** which says,

" By this all men will know that you are my disciples, if you love one another."

clearly commands us to love
one another, His part is to make
it possible in our inner being
and our part is to step out in
dependence upon His enabling
power and act in love. To love
requires decision and action.
The Holy spirit can help a
person to love with agape love
but the person will have to
exercise his will and take the
loving action before he loves
and as he does this always, with
time becomes a truly loving
person and he has the
characteristic of love which is
one of the nine characteristics
of the fruit of the Holy spirit fully
developed in his life. How the
aspect of love can be
developed in the life of a
person is applicable to the

other aspects of the fruit of the holy spirit. The key to developing the fruit of the Holy spirit which any person who wants to develop it must note is to learn to stay in a relationship with Christ. The relationship should be such that the spirit is most able to do His part and the person to express that relationship through obedient action. This quality relationship is called abiding. Jesus in John 15:5-17 which says,

"I am the vine; you are the branches. If a man remains in me and I in him, he will bear much fruit; apart from me you can do nothing. If anyone does not remain in me, he is like a branch that is thrown away and withers; such

branches are picked up,
thrown into the fire and
burned. If you remain in me
and my words remain in you,
ask whatever you wish, and it
will be given you. This is to
my Father's glory, that you
bear much fruit, showing
yourselves to be my disciples.

 "As the Father has loved me,
so have I loved you. Now
remain in my love. If you obey
my commands, you will
remain in my love, just as I
have obeyed my Father's
commands and remain in his
love. I have told you this so
that my joy may be in you and
that your joy may be complete.
My command is this: Love
each other as I have loved you.
Greater love has no one than

this, that he lay down his life for his friends. You are my friends if you do what I command. I no longer call you servants, because a servant does not know his master's business. Instead, I have called you friends, for everything that I learned from my Father I have made known to you. You did not choose me, but I chose you and appointed you to go and bear fruit — fruit that will last. Then the Father will give you whatever you ask in my name. This is my command: Love each other.

 Clearly brings out to us these facts that, if we abide in Him and He in us, we will bear much fruit, which is the fruit of the Holy spirit and abiding in Him is all about obeying His commandments, which we are told in the same passage as to love each other.

From what I have discussed above it is clear that to develop the fruit of the Holy Spirit is a partnership between God and man. A person is able to develop the fruit through exercise or training. There are things which a person must do to be positioned for Gods grace to reach us and change us. Studies have revealed that for a person to develop the fruit of the Holy spirit he will have to practice what I will call **disciplines** and there are **spiritual** and **physical disciplines.**

From all that I have discussed above I am sure you now know how a person can acquire the personal qualities and competencies he needs to be able to live and fulfill his God ordained life purpose. The questions that I believe you are asking which we must answer at this point to be able to come up with the complete strategy for successful living are, how can a person discover his God ordained life purpose? How does he find, create and do what can enable him live and create the value that can enable him to live and fulfill his God ordained life purpose in a God honoring way?

If you will want to know how to discover your God ordained life

purpose and how to find, create
and do what can enable you
live to fulfill it then follow me to
the next chapter.

7:00 HOW TO DISCOVER YOUR GOD ORDAINED LIFE PURPOSE or Calling

Permit me to start the discussion of this subject with the following questions;

what is a life purpose or calling?

what is your God ordained life purpose?

how does a person fulfill it?

how does a person find and create what to do to fulfill it?

Your life calling or purpose* is what you have been created by God to do. (*I have in the discussion in the remaining part of this book taken the words calling and purpose to mean the same so I will be using them interchangeably)

The Bible is very clear about the fact that God created every human being with a unique individual purpose and all humans with a universal purpose. This universal purpose is what most people today refer to as God's universal calling for all humans, which is what they are expected to fulfill while they are in the World. A human being gets to live and fulfill this universal calling by discovering his individual calling, finds what to do to fulfill it and he lives and do it.

The following verses bring out these facts about humans

having individual and universal purposes very clearly.

The confirmation that every human being has a unique individual purpose is revealed in,

(a) **Jeremiah 1:5**

"Before I formed thee in the belly, I knew thee ;and before thou comest forth out of the womb I sanctified thee ,and I ordained thee a prophet unto the nations."

(b)**Judges 13:5**

"For ,lo, thou shalt conceive ,and bear a son and no razor shall come on his head ,for the child shall be a Nazarite unto God from the womb and he shall

begin to deliver Israel out of the hand of the Philistines."

(c) **Exodus 9:16**

"And in very deed for this cause have I raise thee up ,for to show in thee my power and that my name may be declared throughout all the earth."

The confirmation that God created all humans with a universal purpose is revealed in

(c) Genesis 1:26 tells us why God created man.

"And God said let us make man in our image in our likeness and let them have dominion over the fish of the sea and over the fowl of the air and over the cattle and over all the earth and over every

creeping thing that creepeth upon the earth."

(d)Romans 8:29 tells us that God has called all people to become like His son Jesus Christ.

"For whom He did foreknow, He also did predestinate to be conformed to the image of His Son ..."

As I said earlier studies revealed that it is when a person lives and fulfills his individual purpose that he fulfills the universal purpose of man

The need for all people to know their lives purposes and be able to live and   fulfill them as I said earlier is based on the fact

that life is a TRUST and it must
be stewarded faithfully(used for
the purpose that it is meant for)
for it to be a success. Achieving
a truly successful life by a
person is therefore all about
the person discovering his life
purpose, finding what to do to
fulfill it, develop or train himself
to acquire the dispositions and
competencies he needs to be
able to live and do this thing
that can enable him to live and
fulfill his purpose in
accordance with God's will or
in a God honoring way.

How a person can discover his
life purpose, find what he can
do to fulfill it and how he
should live and develop himself
to acquire all that he needs to
be able to become able to do

this thing that he needs to do to fulfill his life purpose are discussed in the remaining part of this book.

How a person can go about doing these things which have been discussed and explained in details in the remaining parts of this book are important especially for you a Christian as it is only when a person is able to live and fulfill his life calling in a God honoring way that he can live and experience a truly fulfilling enjoyable and prosperous life and having a successful life so read on.

why most people are not able to live and fulfill their lives purposes.

Permit me to take some time to explain why most people are unable to live and fulfill their lives purposes before we look at how a person can live and discover his life purpose Studies have revealed that most people living today are not able to live and fulfill their lives purposes because they do not know them and where they do they do not know how to live and fulfill them. It has been discovered that there are also cases where people know their lives callings and how to live and fulfill them but they never get to live and fulfill them. The studies revealed that the reason is that, they are not people who can live to; they do not have the requirements for living and fulfilling their lives purposes.

Research revealed that this problem of inability to live and fulfill life purpose by most people even when they know their purposes and how to live and fulfill them is because of the fact that it has always been wrongly seen and generally held by most people that for a person to be able to live and fulfill his individual life purpose and his universal purpose as a human being, all he needs is for him to,

i Know the purpose.

ii, Know the right work which when done enables him to live out the purpose.

iii, Know and acquire the requirements for doing this work that he needs to do to fulfill his life purpose.

The requirements for doing work successfully are usually seen by most people to only be the skills a person needs to do the work.

Studies have however revealed that only knowing one's life purpose and the details of the work that when done enables a person to fulfill his life purpose and acquiring the skills which such a person needs to do this work which enables him fulfill what he has been created to do are not enough for a person to live and do this work successfully.

The studies revealed that a person will need to have some additional requirements for him to be able to live and do the work that can enable him live to fulfill his individual life purpose and achieve the universal purpose of human beings successfully. It is actually the inability of most people to know and have these additional requirements after they have known and acquired the details about their lives purposes and requirements for living to fulfill life purpose that most people have been unable to live and fulfill their individual purposes and achieve man's universal purpose.

I will therefore want us to start our journey to discovering our lives purposes and how to live and fulfill them with the knowledge of the additional requirements that a person needs and how to acquire them.

These additional requirements have been found to be,

(i The person must become the person who can live and do the work which when done in accordance with god's will enables him to fulfill his life purpose .

(ii) The person must be able to live, acquire and use (steward) faithfully (while doing the work which when done enables him to fulfill his life purpose and achieve what he has been called to be and do) adequate quantities of the resources that he needs to meet his basic needs adequately to be free and fit to live and fulfill his life purpose. Most people are not able to live and do what they should do to fulfill their lives purposes because they are not free and fit to do so. The struggle for what they need to survive and how they live, get things, relate to these things they get and people prevents them from being free and fit to live and do successfully what they should do to fulfill their lives purposes.

The questions that come out from the above things that I have discussed which we will need to answer to know what a person's purpose is, what he needs to have ,who he needs to become to do the work that enables him to live and fulfill his life's purpose to achieve his individual and universal purposes as a human being are the following,

i How does a person discover **his individual calling?**

ii What does it mean to *become ?*

     iii Why does a person need to *become* before he can do the

     work he has been called to do?

     iv How does a person *become?*

v What are these *resources* that a person needs to meet his basic needs to be free and fit to live and do the things that enables him to fulfill his calling ?

vi Why does a person need these *resources*?

vii How does a person live to acquire these **resources?**

8:00 WHY YOU NEED TO LIVE AND FULFILL YOUR LIFE PURPOSE.

Before we answer the questions that we ended the last chapter with, I will want to take some time to further clarify and bring out very clearly why it is important that every person must and should be able to discover his life calling, find the work to do which can enable him fulfill it, do everything possible to develop himself to acquire all that he needs to live and do this work effectively so that he can live out his life calling successfully.

Every human being needs to know his life calling and should be able to live and fulfill or achieve it because if he does not many things will happen. Prominent amongst these things that will happen are,

(i) his life will be unfulfilling, meaningless and unsatisfactory.

Fulfillment, meaning and satisfaction in life is experienced by a person only when such a person knows his life calling and lives for the fulfillment of this calling which God created him for. Studies revealed that a person will thrive in a location and vocation with joy and personal growth and feeling satisfied because of the difference his work makes only at his place of calling

(ii) he will live in lack(poverty) of all the resources that he needs to meet his basic needs. This will lead to him not being fit and free to live, do what he needs to do to fulfill his life's purpose and enjoy a good quality life.

This is because all the resources that a person needs to live, meet his basic needs to be free to do what will enable him fulfill his life calling, have been promised and provided for by God but he can have access to them only when he has a healthy relationship with God and is living in obedience to Him and fulfilling his calling in life.

(iii) the destinies of many people which depend on the Person living and fulfilling his callings will remain unfulfilled.

The inability of people to live and fulfill their life calling will lead to society remaining unchanged and suffering from lack and underdevelopment as it is the fulfillment of lives callings by people in a society that brings about changes and progress to a society. God partners with people to bring blessings to people and creations through such people being able to live and fulfill their lives purposes.

(iv) society will remain in bondage to Satan, his agents and circumstances like poverty, sicknesses etc that they bring on people.

Experience has revealed that a society remains in bondage to Satan and his agents through the circumstances that they bring upon it unless the people who live there are able to do the works that they have been called to do effectively. The change which we are today craving for or desiring in our societies and indeed the world, cannot be brought about by politicians or Government through legislation, it will take place only through helping people to become able to live and fulfill their lives callings.

9:00 HOW TO ACQUIRE THE REQUIREMENTS THAT A PERSON NEEDS TO LIVE AND FULFILL HIS LIFE PURPOSE.

From what I have discussed above you will agree with me that it is important and necessary for all people to be helped to discover their lives callings, develop themselves to acquire the dispositions and competencies they require for successful living, find what to do to be able to live and fulfill them. It is when they have these requirements that they can acquire the things they need to overcome all that can stop them from living to fulfill their lives callings.

Studies have revealed to us
that answering the questions we
had listed and ended the last
chapter with can enable a
person to know how to live and
acquire these requirements
needed for fulfilling a calling.
Answering the questions will
enable a person to know how to
become and how to live and
do what he needs to do to be
able to live and overcome all
that can stop a person from
living to fulfill his life calling.

I will therefore want us to
answer these questions.

(a) HOW DOES A PERSON DISCOVER HIS LIFE PURPOSE ?

If a person wants to discover his life purpose, he will have to begin his search with God. This is because God created all human beings and He made each for a purpose which only Him knows exactly what it is. This means that, if a person wants to know his life's purpose he must believe that God created him for a unique purpose and so to know it he will have to ask God who created him. When a person ask God for what his life purpose is, God will reveal it to him.

There are however things that God has put in place which such a person can use as a guide or means for confirming what his life calling is after he has asked God to reveal it to him. Prominent amongst these things that God has put in human beings which a person who wants to know his life purpose can use to know what his life purpose is are his gifts. Studies revealed that every human being is born with gifts. God in His wisdom has put in people when He created them what can enable them to be able to live and fulfill their lives purposes. He equips each person with specific gifts which are related to his purpose. An important key to discovering your life purpose can therefore be found in discovering the gifts God has given you. Your gifts can tell and help you understand your life purpose and so you can get to be sure about your life purpose by asking and answering the following questions,

(i)what has God gifted me to do?

(ii)what am I good at doing?

(iii) what gets me excited? When something energizes you and causes you to be excited, it is certain that it is related to your gift and to your purpose.

When you are able to determine your gift and you begin to operate in it, you will have direction in your life and you will begin to move towards your life purpose which will in turn provide you with direction to your destiny. It is important for you to know that your purpose does not contain the specifics of your destiny, but knowing it will enable you take the right direction to what the specifics are for your life. A case in point which I will want to use as an example is the case of Joseph in the Bible. Joseph had a dream from God and it gave him vision and direction in his life, but he didn't know what the final manifestations of that dream would look like. Joseph also had a gift God gave him and that gift gave him purpose in his everyday life, but he didn't know the specifics of how that gift would be used in his destiny. It is obvious that Joseph had a gift of administration, this can be seen in the fact that while he was a slave in Potiphar's house he organized the house so well that he became overseer of the house and when he was in the prison, he also organized the prison so well that he became an overseer of the prison. Joseph understood that he had a gift of administration and was faithful to use that gift wherever he went. Joseph however did not know the specifics of how that gift would play a part in his destiny. His destiny was what his life was meant for and all he went through in his life turned

out to have been preparation
and avenue for development
for him to become a person
who can fulfill his life purpose.

 In the same way, when you
discover your gift you may not
know what exactly God has
created you to be and do with it
but your faithful use of it will
take you to your destiny.

A persons gifts point to what he
has been created to do as they
reveal what the person can do.
In the same way your life
assignment is revealed by your
gifts. Discover your gifts and
you will discover your life
purpose.

 People can also be a source of
confirming to you what you
have been called to be and do.

People can do this because they see you and can tell what gifts you have through their observation of who you and what you can do well.

(b)WHAT DOES IT MEAN TO BECOME?

After a person has known his life calling, he will need to become a person who can live and do the work that he needs to do to fulfill it before he can. To **become** means to acquire personal qualities(character traits) and competencies. When we talk of a person becoming a person who can do the work he needs to do to be able to live and fulfill his life calling we are talking of him acquiring the **personal qualities and**

competencies he needs to discipline, order and manage himself to be able to live and practice the disciplines necessary to do the work such a person needs to do to fulfill what he has been called to do.

Becoming is therefore about acquiring **dispositions and competencies**.

(c) *WHY DOES A PERSON NEED TO BECOME BEFORE HE CAN DO ANYTHING SUCCESSFULLY?*

A person needs to and must **become** before he can do anything especially what he has been created and called to do

successfully because,
becoming enables a person to,

(i) develop the commitment and acquire the character and competencies needed to do the work which he has been called to do.

(ii) acquire the capacity and competencies needed to receive and manage faithfully the results of his work. This is very necessary as things attract things. When a person does not have this capacity and competencies he stands to even be destroyed by the proceeds or results of his work. e.g. money attracts things to whoever gets money and as such whoever wants money must first make sure he acquires the capacity(which character gives) and competencies(which skills give) to deal with these things that money attracts and manage money faithfully before he goes after money.

1Timothy 6:9 confirms to us this fact that money attracts things to whoever gets money,

"But they that will be rich fall into temptation and a snare, and into many foolish and hurtful lusts which drown men in destruction and perdition."

(iii) acquire the capacity to overcome the hindrances that Satan can place on a persons way to living out his calling . There are hindrances to everything a person wants to do or get in the world. These hindrances are internal (inside him) and external (in his environment and others)

(iv)acquire the ability to control, discipline and manage himself to practice the disciplines needed for doing the work that he needs to do to enable him fulfill his life purpose or calling.

(v)acquire the ability to be able to live and be fit for the race of life.

The need to become before a person can do has been discovered and it is being used by institutions like the **ARMY**. This is why the Army never assigns a recruit army work until he has gone through the depot where he is made to become a soldier.

Jesus did also employ this approach of **becoming** before **doing** in **His** ministry.

In **Matthew 4:19,** we read that when Jesus called His first disciples they were fishermen, but for them to be able to do the new work of, *"fishing men"* which He was calling them to ,He said they will first have to be made fishers of men before they fish men. This is because fishing "fish" is different from fishing "men"

"And he said unto them, follow me and I will make you fishers of men."

This principle of you must become before you can do is key. It is what people need to be able to do whatever they want to do. This is because, people do things because of **who they are and not because of what skills they have or what they know**.

What you do reveal who you are, just as a tree's fruit reveals the type of a tree it is. A tree produces fruit after its type. A good tree produces good fruit and a bad tree produces bad fruit.

To change what a person does or what a person can do you will need to change who he is.

Not including how to become in our approach to training

people to do things has been the missing link in our training programs, hence people trained in our training programs never get to be able to do what they are trained to do.

(d) **HOW DOES A PERSON BECOME**

A person becomes by changing his **dispositions (character), competencies(skill) and lifestyle.**

A persons character is revealed by his habits, so to change a persons character change his **habits**.

Habits are formed through what a person does regularly . This means if you can get a person to do something over and over , he will develop a habit from it. e.g. Tell lies often and you become a liar.

Changing a person will therefore require that he schedules activities which when done regularly enables the person to develop the habits that doing those activities result in their acquisition .Becoming is the result of doing. No one wakes up and find that he has become without first having been involved in doing the things that enable him to acquire the character traits he needs to become. Becoming require regular practice or exercise. Apostle Paul reveals to us the secret of how to become in **1Timothy 4:7**.Where he advised Timothy about how to become godly. He told him if he wants to become godly he should, "... **exercise himself unto godliness**." Godliness is acquired through exercise or training.

(e) *HOW TO LIVE TO BECOME WHO YOU NEED TO BECOME TO DO THE WORK THAT WILL ENABLE YOU TO FULFILL YOUR LIFE PURPOSE.*

For you to live and become the person that you need to become to be able to live and fulfill your life purpose will require that you change your lifestyle and the things you do and how you do them. For this to happen, there are areas of your life which you must focus at and develop in order to **become this person that** you need to **become to have** what you need to have to be able to live and do the work that will enable you live and do what you have been created to do.

The areas are the following,

(i) The first area of life you must focus at is **personal development**.

This has to do with the development or growth of your character, physical fitness and wellness, wisdom and competence (skills).

(ii)The second area of your life that you must focus at are your relationships. Man exist in **relationships** so this has to do with creating and having in a healthy condition all the relationships that all humans exist in.

Man exist in relationships and fulfills his purpose through relationships and as such you will be able to live and fulfill your life calling only when you are able to do the things that enables you to create and maintain in a healthy condition all these relationships that all humans exist in and you are in.

(iii) The third area of life you must focus at is **life purpose or calling fulfillment**.

 This has to do with you finding what to do which when done

enables you to fulfill your life purpose. You must therefore develop yourself to acquire the characteristics and skills you need to do this work well and you live to do it while living your life. This will enable you to live a life of purpose focused at your purpose fulfillment.

What the above are saying is that, for a person to live and become who he needs to become to do what he needs to do to fulfill his life purpose, it is required that such a person lives a God centered balanced life of purpose which is focused at doing the things that enable him achieve the three things listed above.

However for a person to be able to live this way and achieve all the above, he will need to change. For a person to change he needs God to change him as no human being can change himself. For him to be positioned where God can reach and change him he will need to be born again, live life based on God's word under the guidance of the Holy Spirit, practice spiritual disciplines which are Gods means of grace. For a person to do these he will need to discipline himself, live and order his life in such a way that he allocates his time for these things that he needs to do to develop himself to achieve or do the three things discussed above regularly.

(f) WHAT ARE THE RESOURCES THAT A PERSON NEEDS TO BE ABLE TO LIVE AND DO THE WORK THAT ENABLES HIM TO LIVE OUT HIS LIFE PURPOSE SUCCESSFULLY.

The resources that a person needs for him to be able to live be free and fit to do what he needs to do to live out his life purpose through doing the work that enables him to live out his life purpose are the resources that all human beings need to meet their **basic human needs.** All human beings are born with three basic needs. It is only when these needs are being met adequately and correctly(God's way) by a person as he lives that such a person becomes free and fit to be able to live, do what he needs to do to fulfill his life calling successfully and experience a satisfactory, meaningful and impactful life which we call a successful life.

Experience has revealed that the quality of a persons life is dependent on who he is(character) and the degree to which such a person is able to meet his basic needs correctly. Being able to do this frees him up and makes him fit to be able to live and do what he needs to do to fulfill his life purpose. Many people living today are not able to live correctly and fulfill their lives purposes because they lack the required commitment, character traits and competencies(skills, knowledge) and fitness to live and do what they need to do to fulfill their life purposes. For details of what it means to be fit for the race of life and how to be fit please read my book titled ARE YOU FIT FOR THE RACE OF LIFE.

The lack of the resources people need for meeting their basic needs has also contributed in preventing them from living to fulfill their lives callings as it leads to them not only being free and fit to be focused at doing what they need to do to fulfill their lives purposes but they get distracted. Studies revealed that most people are not able to live and fulfill their lives purposes because they are being tied down in life by the burden of the consequences of wrong living which results in people not being able to make progress in any area of their lives and their lives ending up as merely a struggle for survival. These peoples lives and endeavors are focused at nothing but survival.

(g)WHAT ARE THESE BASIC NEEDS THAT ALL HUMANS

HAVE AND MUST MEET ADEQUATELY TO BE FREE AND FIT TO LIVE LIFE SUCCESSFULLY ?

All humans are created with three basic needs. These three basic human needs that every human being have, exist at the three levels that man exist, spirit, soul and body.

There is a need at each level and they are as follows,

(i) spiritual at the spirit level

(ii) emotional at the soul level

(iii) physical at the physical level

(h) WHAT ARE THE RESOURCES THAT A PERSON NEEDS FOR MEETING THESE BASIC NEEDS AND WHAT ARE THEIR SOURCES ?

The resources that are needed for meeting these basic needs are as follows

(i) spiritual need

The resource needed for meeting this need is spiritual fulfillment.

God is the source of this resource

ii) Soul or social need

The resource needed for meeting this need is peace of mind. It has to do with the emotions of a person. The source of this resource is God through people.

(iii) Physical need

The resource needed for meeting this need is material things. These are mostly things that money can buy.

The source of this resource is God but He gets it to those who need them through people. You get things money through people by serving them in the marketplace where the exchange of goods and services takes place.

(i) HOW DOES A PERSON LIVE TO, BECOME AND ACQUIRE THESE RESOURCES THAT HE NEEDS TO MEET HIS BASIC NEEDS .

All the training or development that a person needs to become and the resources that he needs to meet the three basic needs that he has can be acquired through **work that he can do using his gifts to,**

(i) serve people through rendering a service

(ii) meet a need through the production of a product or solve a problem in their lives.

 For him to be able to serve people through the work he does well, he will need to have all the relationships that he exist in (Studies have revealed that life for all humans is lived in relationships) must be in a healthy condition. Relationships are created and are maintained in a healthy condition only if they are created and are being run based on God's principles for relationships .This means for a person to live, to become who he has been called to become, acquire and use correctly(inline with God's principles of stewardship) adequate quantities of these resources that he needs to meet his basic needs and be free to live and fulfill his life calling, he must have the right type of work and he must work correctly(Working correctly means working in line with God's principles and purpose for work) and all the relationships that he exist in as a human being in a healthy condition.

The questions that come up as a result of these truths are,

(j) How do all the things I have described above happen or take place?

(ii) What is this right work for a person and how does such a

person find and select this right
work which when done is able
to enable him become who he
has been called to become,
acquire the resources he needs
to meet his basic needs, create
and sustain in healthy condition
the relationships that he exist in
as a human being and be free
to do the work that enables him
to fulfill his life calling?

A person **becomes** through the
work he does because as he
works in his work his work
,works on him. e.g. As a mason
builds a house the house builds
the mason. This happens as he
interacts with people and
things as he builds. The process
helps him to develop his
character and skills resulting in
him becoming both a better

mason and person at the end of the building project.

Studies have however revealed that this can be realized only if he is born again and had been able to use God's principles as his guide in the interactions as he built.

For the work which the person can do for these to happen it must be the right work for him. The right work for a person is the work that enables him to do what he has been called to do. This work is that which he can do using his talents and gifts to serve his fellow man. He can find this work by identifying his life calling(The human problem that he has been equipped to solve), talents, gifts, skills and what he can do(job or business) using these attributes.

The relationships that all humans exist in and the resources that are acquired through each of them are as follows,

(i) *Relationship with God.*

The resource that is acquired through this relationship is spiritual fulfillment. For a person to acquire this resource which is needed for meeting the spiritual need of a person he must have a healthy relationship with God.

(ii)*Relationship with self*

The resource that is acquired through this relationship is a healthy emotional state. This results from peace of mind which comes from having a healthy self worth.

(iii) *Relationship with others*

The resources that are acquired through this relationship are two in number, they are a healthy emotional state and access to financial resources which are needed for the acquisition of material things needed for meeting physical needs. Access to financial resources gives a person the opportunity to use them and be trained in stewardship resulting in the acquisition of stewardship skills which every person needs for him to be entrusted with resources by

God. Interaction with people also leads to character training.

These resources enable a person to be free and fit to live and do the work that enables him live out his calling successfully.

For a person to be able to live,

 (i) Find and do successfully the right work for him which can enable him do what he has been created to do, become who he has been called to be and be able to acquire all the resources that he needs to live out his life calling.

(ii) Create and maintain in a healthy condition the relationships he lives in, the person will have to be born again become truly empowered economically and is able to live the lifestyle of people who are born again and are truly empowered economically.

The question is,

(a)What does it mean to be born again and truly empowered economically?

(b)How does a person become born again and truly empowered economically?

(c)What is the lifestyle of people who are born again and are truly empowered economically ?

- *What does it mean to be born again?*

To be born again means to accept Jesus Christ as ones Lord and Savior

- **What does it mean to be truly empowered economically?**

To truly empower a person economically means to enable such a person through education and training to acquire the required mindset and competencies that can enable such a person to live a life of effective participation in the economy. A life of effective participation in the economy by a person is a life of useful contribution to the economy and benefiting from the economy of the community a person lives in. A person is said to be making a useful contribution to the economy of his community, when he is able to live a productive and profitable life in his community. He is benefitting when he is able to earn an adequate income from the economy. This is best done by a person when he is able to know his calling, develop himself , acquire the mindset and skills that enables him to serve people through providing a service or producing a product which solves a problem or meet a need of the people in his community, nation or the world as a whole.

A person that is born again and is truly empowered economically and is living a truly economically empowered lifestyle will,

(a) know and understand his life calling.

(b)live his daily life such that he is daily developing himself and acquiring the mindset of the kingdom of God citizens and skills of people who live godly , productive and profitable lifestyles.

This is because all those that are born again and are truly empowered economically live godly, productive and profitable lifestyles.

(c) be involved daily in activities that enables him to be living out his calling. These activities must be done in accordance with God's will and profitably.

Living out life this way will not only enable him to do the work which enables him fulfill his life calling effectively according to God's will but he will also be able to,

(a) work to empower others to become born again, truly empowered economically and are able to live godly and truly economically empowered lifestyles

(b) regularly relate to people thereby having the opportunity to serve them and also train himself in creating and maintaining healthy relationships.

(c) have the opportunity to develop his character as he relates with people regularly.

(d) has the opportunity to work in a godly way and acquire the resources he needs to meet his three basic needs God's way as living a godly truly economically empowered lifestyle will require that a person relates correctly (God's way) with all the sources of the three basic needs.

Based on what I have discussed above I am sure you will agree with me if I say that a person can not live and fulfill his life calling correctly(God's way) unless he becomes born again and truly empowered economically . This is because from what we have discussed, it is clear that becoming, born again and truly empowered economically enables a person to be able to live a godly and productive lifestyle .He will also be able to live and order his life in a way that he is able to attend to all areas of his life correctly(God's way), adequately and has a balanced life. He will also because of this be able to acquire all the resources he needs to meet all his basic needs adequately and be free from hindrances that can prevent a person from being able to live for life calling fulfillment and is able to live and do the work that enables him fulfill his life calling according to God's will and experience a good quality life.

The questions that we will need to answer at these stage for us to conclude our discussion on why true economic empowerment is necessary for a Person   to be able to live and do the work which he has been created to do to fulfill his life calling,

(i) How does a Person become truly empowered economically?

(ii) What are the steps that he should follow?

(iii) What is the lifestyle of a person who is truly empowered

economically?

(iv) How does this lifestyle enable him to do the work that enables him to fulfill his life purpose?

(K)HOW DOES A PERSON BECOME TRULY EMPOWERED ECONOMICALLY .

For a person to become truly economically empowered it will require that he acquires the mindset and skills of people who are truly economically empowered which have been found to be as follows,

(a)The mindset and skills of these people have been found to be as follows;

(i)They have a mindset of abundance, prosperity, productivity and growth. They emphasize true wealth(wealth that has all the three components of spiritual, relational and material) acquisition over just material wealth acquisition as true wealth enables the realization of a good quality life/wellbeing by people

(ii) They have an attitude and mindset which emphasizes the personal development of local wealth producing resources in an area by the people of the area for the fulfillment of their purposes and missions in life rather than waiting for people from outside to come and do it for them

(iii) They have an attitude and mindset that desires and promotes the attainment of prosperity and successful or abundant living by all.

(b) The skills have been found to be as follows

The basic skills needed by those that are truly economically empowered to live a life style of true economic empowerment (these are true wealth creation skills) are as follows;

(i) Relational skills

These are skills that enables a person to create and sustain healthy relationships with others. A person who wants to live a truly economically empowered lifestyle must have these skills.

(ii) Money making skills

These can be classified as, financial literacy, problem solving, communication, marketing and negotiation skills. These can enable a person solve peoples problems, create income sources and be able to earn income always.

(iii) Wealth increasing skills

These can be classified as, leveraging or Investing skills which a person can use to invest a part of the income he earns from the income sources he creates with his money making/wealth creation skills

(iv) Wealth using skills

These can be classified as wealth protection, stewardship or budgeting skills .These are skills which enables a true wealth creator to not waste the wealth he has created and also prevent the wealth he creates from being taken away from him by Satan or his agents in the world and be able to steward it well.

(iv) Wealth distribution skills

These can be classified as wealth sharing and empowerment skills. In Gods kingdom where the skills listed above are the basic skills that every citizen must have to be given access to wealth, every citizen is considered a channel and hence the need for the skills listed here as wealth distribution skills. A part of the true wealth acquired by any citizen of the kingdom of God is expected to be distributed to others. It should be allowed to flow to others to provide for those in need or to empower those who needs empowerment to also become true wealth creators. It is when the citizens of Gods kingdom do this that they are given more true wealth, unlike the kingdom of darkness where every citizen is striving to be a dam (keep or hoard any wealth that come their way).It is because of these practices that in the kingdom of God it is about sowing and reaping while in the kingdom of darkness(Satan) it is about buying and selling(acquiring and keeping all you can get).

The question is how does a person acquire these dispositions and skills?

Going by what we have discussed above it is clear that these dispositions are found only in the kingdom of God so for a person to acquire them he

must first become a citizen of
the kingdom of God. After a
person becomes a citizen of the
kingdom of God by being born
again he will need to follow the
advise Paul gave the Romans
and Timothy when he was
advising them/ him on how to
become transformed and godly
for them/ him to acquire these
dispositions. A person can
acquire these attitudes /
mindsets (dispositions) and
skills and be able to live and do
his life work and fulfill his life
purpose only through training
which leads to mind renewal
and transformation. A person
who wants to become truly
empowered economically must
therefore plan his life, be able
to order and structure his life

such that he lives a balanced life and is able to do regularly the things that he needs to do for his personal development in all areas of his life thereby acquires the disposition and skills he needs to be truly empowered economically and be able to live the lifestyle of such people.

(L)HOW A PERSON CAN LIVE TO ACQUIRE THESE MINDSETS AND SKILLS

As I said earlier a person becomes through training and practice. Nobody **becomes** by wishing or the laying of hands as becoming results from the acquisition of character traits and competencies which are the revelation of habits and skills. Habits and skills are acquired from things a person does regularly.

Studies have revealed to us that for a person to live and acquire these habits which translates into character traits he will need to live godly and in **a balanced way**.

Living a balanced life or living in a balanced way means living in such a way that he is able to discipline himself and give adequate attention to every area/dimension of his life that makes up his life.

These areas of life which he must give attention to can be grouped into three main groups as follows, i Personal development

ii Relationships

iii Purpose fulfillment

The question is,

What will enable a person to live a balanced life that enables him to be able to live, attend to each of these three areas of his life regularly, adequately, correctly and effectively to enable him develop them well and be well equipped to live and fulfill his life calling successfully?

For a person to live a balanced life and be able to attend to every area of his life regularly, correctly and effectively to develop them and be able to live out his life calling successfully and experience a good quality life, he will need to,

(i) Develop a life plan and live by it.

A life plan enables a person to plan how to live his life well by prioritizing and scheduling his daily activities such that he is able to allocate time to every activity in each area/dimension of his life so that he is able to attend to every area of his life regularly, effectively and correctly. A person will be able to live a balanced life only if he can plan his life and live by the plan.

For how to do this you can get details and if possible try to participate in our **life planning/coaching workshop titled,**

WIN@LIFE WIN@WORK .

Efficient Research Dynamic Jos, Plateau State, Nigeria.

Phone: +2348107996660

Email: info@erdworld.com

www.ingramcontent.com/pod-product-compliance
Lightning Source LLC
Chambersburg PA
CBHW051652170526
45167CB00001B/439